To Janice

All the best for your birthday

Paul

SPILL THE BEANS

David Harmer
Paul Cookson

a twist in the tale

1996

"SPILL THE BEANS"
First published January 1993 by
"A Twist in the Tale"
P.O. Box 25, Retford Road, Notts. DN22 7ER
2nd Edition published August 1993
3rd Edition published December 1994
4th Edition published March 1996
ISBN 1 874335 03 6

Copyright Paul Cookson and David Harmer 1993

All poems written Paul Cookson and David Harmer

All illustrations, artwork and layout Paul Cookson

David wrote the poem "Trainspotter" with his friend Martyn Wiley who died in 1994

Photographs by Steven McKay

Printed by Herbert Robinson
Elizabeth Court, Manners Industrial Estate,
Ilkeston, Derbyshire. Tel: 0115 944 2063

Special Thanks to:-
Andy Camp's Android Vampire Hamster, Karen Bell, Nick Toczek and Greenbelt Festivals

CONTENTS

Pumping Iron	by David and Paul	1
Big Bad Barry The Bully	by David and Paul	2
Barry's Budgie	by David	3
Mum Used Prittstick	by Paul	4
The Dinosaurs That Time Forgot	by David and Paul	5
I Like Insects	by David	6
Arnies Films : One	by David and Paul	7
Born In Widnes	by David and Paul	8
I Want I Want I Want	by David and Paul	10
Bessie Is The Boss	by David	12
Camouflage Ken	by David and Paul	13
The Dare	by David	14
The Android Vampire Hamsters	by Paul	16
Unzip Your Lips	by David and Paul	18
Picnic Time On The M25	by Paul	19
Stuck Behind The Man With The Caravan	by David and Paul	20
Bully In A Lorry - Get Out Of My Way	by David and Paul	22
Father's Hands	by Paul	24
Losing At Home	by Paul	26
Winter Morning Winter Night	by David	27
With Her Trolley And Her Brolly And Her Plastic Bags Granny Goes Into Town	by Paul	28
Shirley And Charlotte The Shell Suit Sisters	by Paul	30
F.A. Rules O.K.	by David and Paul	31
Giving Their Goalie Backache	by David	32
The Inventor's House	by David	33
Happy As A Pig In Muck	by Paul	34
From Pontefract To Doncaster	by David	36
Arnies Films : Two	by David and Paul	37
Trainspotter	by David and Martyn	38
The Man With Four Chins	by Paul	40
The Amazing Captain Concorde	by Paul	42
What On Earth Has Happened To My Little Sister Hayley Ann?	by Paul	44
Riboflavin	by David	45
To The Pork Pie	by David	46
What Class Four Fear The Most	by David	47
More Dinosaurs That Time Forgot	by David and Paul	47
Percy Is A Punk Rocker	by Paul	49
Rocker On A Pushbike	by Paul	50

Dedicated to
Lizzie and Harriet
and
Jacqueline Lees

PUMPING IRON

ME AND MY MATE DOWN AT THE GYM
PUMPING IRON KEEPING TRIM
ONE TWO ... PUFF PANT
THREE FOUR ... PUFF PANT
FIVE SIX ... PUFF PANT
SEVEN EIGHT ... FLIPPING HECK
NINE TEN ... NOT AGAIN

We come here twice a week
Working hard on our physique
I come here to pump my iron
I come here with my spare tyre on
My muscle are steel, they've got to be seen
Mine feel like Plasticine

ME AND MY MATE DOWN AT THE GYM ... ETC

I sweat adrenaline pure and hard
I sweat margarine and lard
Fifteen circuits and I want more
I come in the door and fall on the floor
I fight the flab with lots of swimming
I fight the flab and it keeps winning.

ME AND MY MATE DOWN AT THE GYM ... ETC

Press up! Sit up! Pull up! Step up!
Once he gets going he won't let up
Up! Down! Squat! Thrust
What a poser, I've got you sussed
I work on my thighs
I work on my size
Exercise my tri's and bi's
What a blob! What a slob!
The only muscle's in his gob!

ME AND MY MATE DOWN AT THE GYM ... ETC

BIG BAD BARRY THE BULLY

Was tough
The only nine year old Sumo wrestler
In all South London.

He had loads of tattoos
Not the ones you got from a penny bubbly
But real ones done with a needle
Some were done with a needle and thread.
When he ran out of tattoos
His mum sewed anorak badges all over his body
And he could tell exactly were he'd been on holidays.

He'd been to Chester
It was on his chest
Armthorpe - it was on his arm
Headingly - it was on his head
Neasden - it was on his knee
Anklesea - on his ankles
And he'd been to Ramsbottom
But they don't do a badge from there

He took us for a double bullying
Every Wednesday afternoon after sums
Then he'd say
"Come and see my paraquat
It's in a cage at home"

"Isn't that parakeet?"
I'd say softly, not to be heard
You didn't argue with Barry.

Otherwise he'd tie your head in a knot
Stamp on your head
And let his paraquat
Peck tattoos down your arm.

BARRY'S BUDGIE! BEWARE!

Dave's got a dog the size of a lion
Half-wolf, half-mad, frothing with venom
It chews up Policemen and then spits them out
But it's nowt to the Bird I'm talking about.

Claire's got a cat as wild as a cheetah
Scratching and hissing, draws blood by the litre
Jumps high walls and hedges, fights wolves on its own
But there's one tough budgie it leaves well alone.

Murray my eel has teeth like a shark
Don't mess with Murray, he'll zap out a spark
But when Barry's budgie flies over the houses
Murray dips down his lights, blows his own fuses.

This budgie's fierce, a scar down its cheek
Tattoos on its wings, a knife in its beak
Squawks wicked words does things scarcely legal
Someone should tell Barry it's really an eagle.

MUM USED PRITTSTICK

Mum used Prittstick
Instead of lipstick
Then went and kissed my dad.

Two days passed
Both stuck fast
The longest snog they ever had.

THE DINOSAURS THAT TIME FORGOT

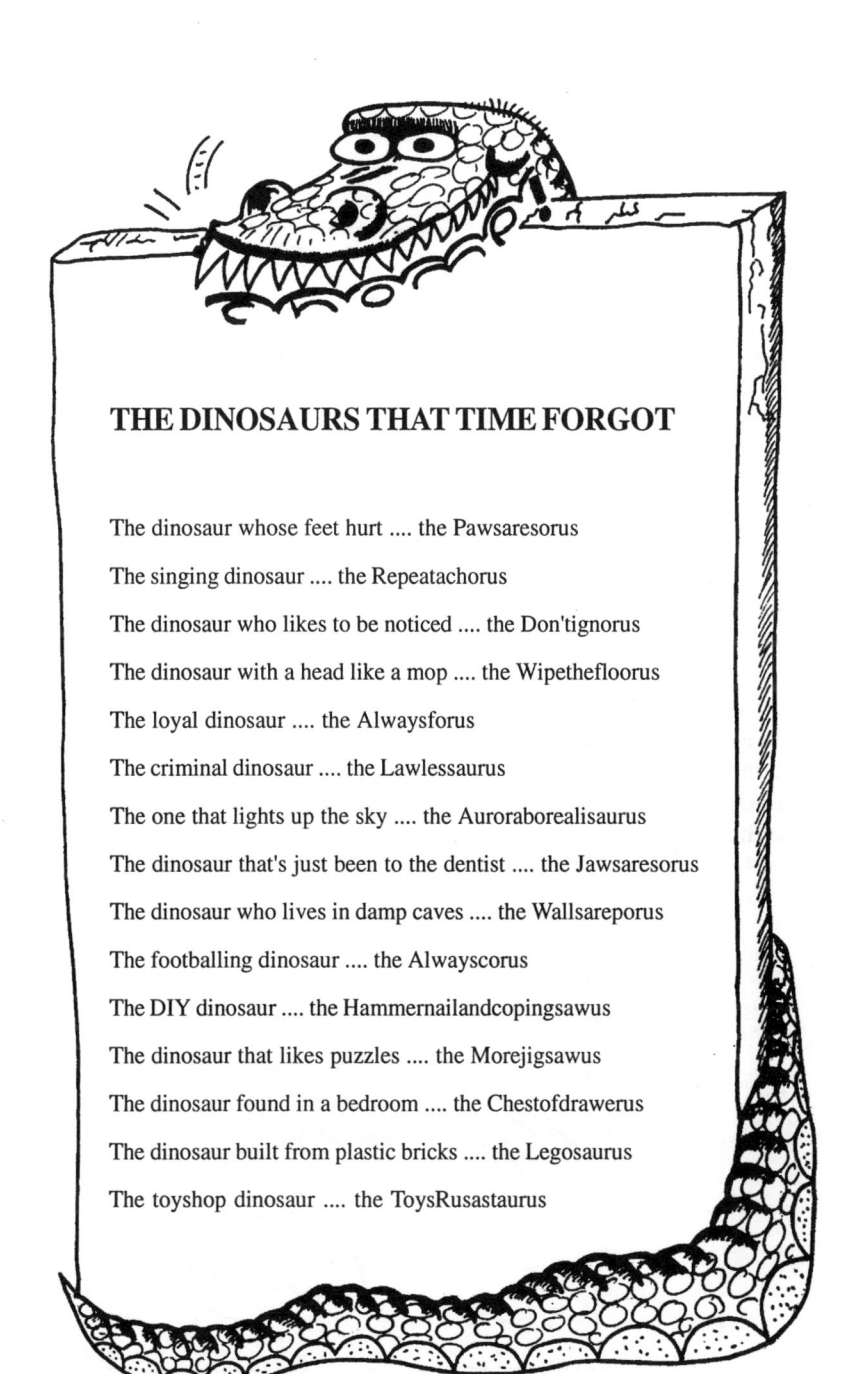

The dinosaur whose feet hurt .... the Pawsaresorus

The singing dinosaur .... the Repeatachorus

The dinosaur who likes to be noticed .... the Don'tignorus

The dinosaur with a head like a mop .... the Wipethefloorus

The loyal dinosaur .... the Alwaysforus

The criminal dinosaur .... the Lawlessaurus

The one that lights up the sky .... the Auroraborealisaurus

The dinosaur that's just been to the dentist .... the Jawsaresorus

The dinosaur who lives in damp caves .... the Wallsareporus

The footballing dinosaur .... the Alwayscorus

The DIY dinosaur .... the Hammernailandcopingsawus

The dinosaur that likes puzzles .... the Morejigsawus

The dinosaur found in a bedroom .... the Chestofdrawerus

The dinosaur built from plastic bricks .... the Legosaurus

The toyshop dinosaur .... the ToysRusastaurus

I LIKE INSECTS

There's some that creep
Some that crawl
But the ones I like the best
Are the icky-sticky prickly ones
I shove down my brother's vest

There's some that fly
Some that buzz
Some that wriggle in the dirt
I like to catch the hairy ones
And drop them down his shirt

When he's asleep on the lawn
His mouth is open wide
I put an earwig on his tongue
Then run away and hide

There's some that sting
Some that bite
Some that itch like a flea
The only insects I don't like
Are the ones he drops on me

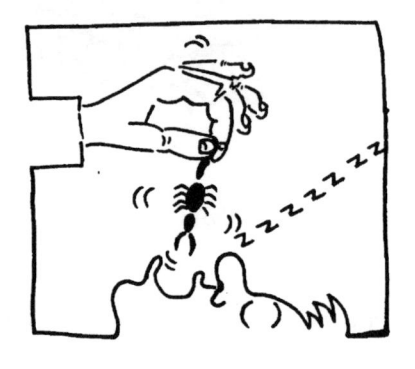

"HAVE YOU SEEN THE FILM WHERE ARNIE STARS AS AN ANDROID CYBORG ALIEN WHO BEAMS DOWN TO A HAIRDRESSERS AND THEN KEEPS ALL THE CUSTOMERS HOSTAGE?"

"NO, WHAT'S IT CALLED?"

"PERMINATOR"

SCHWARZENEGGER

PERMINATOR

BORN IN WIDNES

Gigging in Wigan I get my kicks
Going up North on Route M6
Born in Widnes-mad March morning
Spill The Beans - not dead not boring!
Spill The Beans - not dead not boring!

Retford Sprotbrough Widnes Wigan
These are the places the Beans are big in
Rocking in Runcorn Rolling in Rotherham
Raving in Rochdale we're all over 'em

Barnsley, Derby and Doncaster
No-one does their poems faster
Born in Widnes-they weren't yawning
Spill The Beans - not dead not boring!
Spill The Beans - not dead not boring!

Retford Sprotbrough Widnes Wigan
These are the places the Beans are big in
Rocking in Runcorn Rolling in Rotherham
Raving in Rochdale we're all over 'em

Have Spill The Beans played in the NEC?   No, have we heck!
Have Spill The Beans played Wembley Stadium?   No, have we heck!
Have Spill The Beans played the Sheffield Arena?   No, have we heck!
Have Spill The Beans played the Barnsley Arena?   We might if they build one

Have Spill The Beans played the Lipton Village Festival in a small tin hut on Bodmin moor on a very quiet Easter Sunday?

Yes we have!

Have Spill The Beans played in a tent in a park in Pontefract with one dodgy microphone and a puppeteer who wouldn't get off?

Yes we have!

Have Spill The Beans been banned from a school in Birmingham for saying 'bum' in front of infants?

Yes we have!

Have Spill The Beans played at Morpeth library to a small boy in a Batman suit which he didn't take off not even to laugh which he didn't do much?

Yes we have! Yes we have!
These strange exotic places
With strange exotic faces
Paul and Dave's Antics Roadshow
There's no place that we would not go
Gigs are big gigs are small
Spill The Beans have played them all.

Retford Sprotbrough Widnes Wigan
These are the places
That the Beans are big in
Rocking in Runcorn Rolling in Rotherham
Raving in Rochdale we're all over 'em

A heaving hall couldn't fit any more in
If poems were goals we'd be scoring
No one sleeping no one snoring
Spill The Beans - not dead not boring!
Spill The Beans - not dead not boring!

Parents cheering children roaring
Temperatures and pulses soaring
On the road and always touring
Spill The Beans - not dead not boring!
Spill The Beans - not dead not boring!

The two in Wigan were adoring
Spill The Beans - not dead not boring!

I WANT I WANT I WANT (The Parents' Revenge Poem)

*I want I want I want I want
Gimme that gimme that Pleeaase!
I want I want I want I want
Gimme that gimme that Pleeaase!*

I want a doll I want a bike
And I want a football
I want a CD I want a Gameboy
And I want that video.

Gimme a Mars Bar gimme some crisps
And I want some ice-cream
Gimme a burger gimme some chips
And a big thick milkshake.

*I want I want I want I want
Gimme that gimme that Pleeaase!
I want I want I want I want
Gimme that gimme that Pleeaase!*

Dad Dad I want it now!
Mum Mum I want it now!
Da-ad pleeaase! No Way!
Mu-um pleeaase! No Way!

**We're not made of money
It does not grow on trees
We're sick of all your mithering
And our demands are these**

*We want we want we want we want
Give us this give us this pleeaase!
We want we want we want we want
Give us this give us this pleeaase!*

We want peace we want quiet
And we'd like a lie in
We want rest we want sleep
We want our bedroom tidy!
We're sick of all those Rangers

Those stupid Power Rangers
We just can't stand those Rangers
And turn that Hi-fi down
Do you call that music?
That noisy modern racket
It's nothing like The Beatles

Postman Pat?	Rubbish
East 17?	Rubbish
Sonic the Hedgehog?	Rubbish
Nintendo?	Rubbish
Andi Peters?	Actually, I quite like Andi Peters

I want a doll	We want peace
I want a bike	We want quiet
I want a football	We want a lie in
I want a CD	We want a rest
I want a Gameboy	We want sleep
I want a video	Clean you bedroom
I want a Mars bar	Fold your clothes up
I want crisps	Do the dishes
I want an ice cream	Brush your teeth
I want a burger	Do your homework
I want chips	Tidy your school bag
I want a milkshake	Get out of my sight
I want it now I want it now	Out of my sight Out of my sight
I want it now I want it now	I've had him up to here
I want it now I want it now	All he ever says is
I want it now I want it now	All he ever says is
I want it now I want it now.	

I want I want I want I want
Gimme that gimme that Pleeaase!
I want I want I want I want
Gimme that gimme that Pleeaase!

BESSIE IS THE BOSS

Bessie is the boss Bessie is the boss
Bessie is the boss in our house !
Bessie is the boss Bessie is the boss
Bessie is the boss in our house !
She screams until she's blue (clap clap !)
She yells and stamps her shoe (stomp stomp !)
She won't do a thing we tell her
Oh what can we do coz
Bessie is the boss Bessie is the boss
Bessie is the boss in our house !
Bessie is the boss Bessie is the boss
Bessie is the boss in our house !

If we say left she says right.
If we say up she says down.
If we say day she says night
If we say square she says round.
If we say stop she says go.
If we say green she says red.
If we say high she says low
If we say table she says bed.

Bessie is the boss ... etc.

The other day we had to wear
three cracked eggs in our hair.
After that we had to eat
rotten cheese that stank of feet.
Then Bessie made us drink
washing up water from the sink.
For a laugh we had to try
sloppy slices of mud pie.
We had to stop, we all felt sick.
She began to scream and kick.
The little so and so !
She had heard the dreaded word.
One of us said ... No !

Bessie is the boss ... etc.

If we say Shreddies she says toast.
If we say juice she says water.
We do not brag we do not boast
about the manners of our daughter.
If we say bath she says shower.
If we say young she says old.
We don't argue, don't feel sour
we just do as we've been told !

Bessie is the boss ... etc.

CAMOUFLAGE KEN

CAMOUFLAGE KEN IS SELDOM SEEN
NO-ONE KNOWS WHERE HE HAS BEEN
HE'S AT LARGE IN HIS CAMOUFLAGE
HERE, THERE AND IN BETWEEN
ON THE SCENE, KNOW WHAT I MEAN
EY UP KEN WHERE ARE YOU?

He can change his shape
He can change his size
He can disappear before your very eyes.

He's baffling, he's amazing
His talent is astounding
He can blend in perfectly whatever the surrounding.

CAMOUFLAGE KEN IS SELDOM SEEN ... ETC.

Sometimes he's a table
Sometimes he's a chair
You just thought you saw him
But he wasn't really there.

Sometimes he's a lamp post
Sometimes he's a tree
Sometimes he is soaking
From the passing dogs who ...

CAMOUFLAGE KEN IS SELDOM SEEN ... ETC.

When he was a baby
He hid from his mam disguised as a pram
When he was a lad
A slick manoeuvre - he's the hoover
When he was thirteen
As bedroom door, the things he saw!
Now he has grown up
His infinite ability, his bodily dexterity,
His supple flexibility, remarkable agility,
Chameleon capability, metamorphocility,
Magnificent utility, spatial relativity,
Suspension of reality means
You can't see him easily
No you can't see him easily

CAMOUFLAGE KEN IS SELDOM SEEN ... ETC.

THE DARE

Kev dared us all last Saturday
To hunt the ghost of One-Eyed Jack
The highwayman of Hangman's Wood
But Jacko said he'd hurt his leg
And Carl ran off to meet his mum.

You're scared too Kev said to me
Scared of a ghost, that was it
I got my bike and raced away
Out towards the farms and fields
With Kev right there beside me.

The wood was hanging like a cloud
Low on the skyline, almost there
I heaved the bike across a stile
Began to pedal, saw the bull
A brick wall on four legs charging.

I looked for Kev, but he was off
With the bull not far behind
I pushed the bike into the wood
A cold grey mist began to shimmer
Shadows gathered, I walked on.

I heard the sound of hooves, a cough
Turned and he was there alright
Lace collar, leather boots and cloak
Black mask stretched across his face
One eye blank, his pistol aimed.

Your money or your bike he said
His voice went through me like a sword
He shot a hole in the back tyre
Then disappeared and all I saw
Was an icy cart-track full of puddles.

I got home late, well after dark
I thought my mum and dad would kill me
Claire they yelled where have you been?
I told them but I wasn't heard
They're going to keep me in for weeks.

But none of them could explain
What I'd seen and though they laughed
They could see as well as me
The small hole drilled into the tyre
My strange and ghostly puncture.

THE ANDROID VAMPIRE HAMSTERS

The android vampire hamsters are coming to get you back.
The android vampire hamsters are ready to attack.

They're tired of straw to sleep on.
They're tired of little cages.
They can't stand that little wheel
they run around for ages.

They're sick of nuts and bran.
It doesn't taste that good.
Revenge is on their tiny minds
and now they want your blood because

The android vampire hamsters ... etc.

Their fangs have all been filed
as sharp as razor blades
thanks to the constant gnawing
on the bars upon their cage.

Make sure you're not alone
in the dead of night.
Make sure you cover up your neck.
Don't give then chance to bite.

The android vampire hamsters ... etc.

Look out folks ! Here they come !
They'll nibble your neck and bite your bum.
They're in the sink, they're in the loo
so don't sit down whatever you do.
They sleep in shoes and gobble your toes,
pull the hairs out of your nose.
They run up trouser legs and skirts,
eating underwear and shirts.
They're in your pockets, in your socks,
break down doors and spit out locks.

Everybody's terrified ! When will this nightmare end ?
The android vampire hamsters are out for their revenge !
The android vampire hamsters are out for their revenge !

The android vampire hamsters are coming to get you back.
The android vampire hamsters are ready to attack, attack, attack !

UNZIP YOUR LIPS

Unzip your lips and get to grips
to the beat that skips so let it rip.
Rhyming rhythms for twisting tongues
Gonna rhyme those rhythms all day long.
Gonna roll those rhythms, rhyme those rocks
Gonna twist and tie your tongue in knots.

Goodness gracious! Great balls of fire!
Spill The Beans gonna take you higher!
A wop bop a loo bop a lop bam boom!
Spill The Beans gonna shake the room!
Be bop a lula she`s my baby!
Spill The Beans gonna drive you crazy!
Twist and shout! Shake, rattle and roll!
Okay Beanetttes off you go ...

DOO WOP WOP
BOP BOP SHOWADDYWADDY
A WOP BOP A LOO BOP A LOP BAM BOOM
BABY BABY BABY
WIG WAM BAM BAM SCAM A LAM
TUTTI FRUITY THAT'S ALRIGHT MAMA
WEER ALL CRAZEE NOW! YEAH

Unzip your lips and shake your hips
Spill The Beans' greatest hits
Unroll your tongue, turn up the watts
Unlock the locks in your voice box
Gonna shake your tonsils, rattle your teeth
Roll vocal chords beyond belief

Gonna rock around the clock tonight!
Spill The Beans gonna set your soul alight!
Bless my soul what's wrong with me!
Spill The Beans gonna set you free!
Feel the noize and hit the groove!
Spill The Beans gonna raise the roof!
Twist and shout! Shake, rattle and roll!
Okay Beanettes of you go ...

DOO WOP WOP ... etc

PICNIC TIME ON THE M25

Picnic time go for a ride
set your sights on the countryside
pack the car and start to drive
stop by the side stop by the side
stop by the side of the M25

Deck chairs on the grass verge
Watch the traffic pass NEEOWN!
Try and pour your flask
Ooh ah ooh ooh eeh
Boiling coffee on your knee

Picnic time go for a ride
set your sights on the countryside
pack the car and start to drive
stop by the side stop by the side
stop by the side of the M25

Salmon spread wholemeal bread
Try to eat as you move your head
Left to right try to bite
Ooh ah ooh ooh eeh
Margarine smeared on your knee

Picnic time go for a ride
set your sights on the countryside
pack the car and start to drive
stop by the side stop by the side
stop by the side of the M25

Picnic time on the M25
Toxic gases will collide
Carbon dioxide
Breathe in SNIFF!
Breathe in SNIFF!
Petrol fumes and lead oxide
Cough splutter cough choke
Poisoned lungs are no joke
Ooh ah ooh ooh eeh
Plan your picnics carefully
Seaside or countryside
But don't go down to the M25
Don't go down to the M25
Don't - pic - nic - on - the - M - Twenty -Five!

STUCK BEHIND THE MAN WITH THE CARAVAN

He's stuck
Stuck behind the man
He's stuck
Stuck behind the man
He's stuck
Stuck behind the man
Stuck behind the man with the caravan
Stuck behind the man with the caravan
That's me   ...that's him...

I'm the man with the caravan
    and I'm the man behind
I've got all the weekend
    and I haven't got the time

Bank Holiday country road
caravan with a heavy load
in my mirror I can see
twenty five cars trying to pass me...

I'm two hours late already
I just can't drive this steady
Gotta put my foot down Gotta get past
Gotta get there Gotta get there fast!
Gotta get there Gotta get there fast!

He's stuck ... etc.

Is that a gap in front (gasp!)?
Is that a gap in front (gasp!)?
I'm going to the middle
I'm going to the middle
I'm going to the middle little by little
    I'm trying to overtake it
    I'm trying to overtake it
    I'm trying to overtake it
    I'm never going to make it...

You're stuck...hard luck!
You're stuck...hard luck!

He's stuck ... etc.

A big white "P" in front of me
There's a lay by up ahead
I could make them smile
pull over for a while
but I think I'll
slowly drive five more miles
in style in style instead!

Oh! No! Drat! Blast!
Look at that! He's gone right past!
Goodbye lay by I've gotta drive by
I'm gonna cry if I don't get by
Stuck here til I'm past my sell by
date, I'm late, trying to accelerate
this state is great, this bloke is gonna make me
wait, aggravate, frustrate, agitate, make me hate!

He's stuck ... etc.

Sooner or later sooner or later
he's got to use his indicator
Left or right I don't care
He could go anywhere
Look there! Look there!
He's turning off just there!
Yippee! I'm free!
Open road in front of me
I'll just get round this bend...
Oh no! Not again!

Tough luck, I'm back
I found a short cut down this track
You're stuck, you're stuck
just like you were before
     And I can't stand it any more!

He's stuck
Stuck behind the man
He's stuck
Stuck behind the man
He's stuck
Stuck behind the man
Stuck behind the man with the caravan
Stuck behind the man with the caravan
Stuck behind the man with the
brilliant   ...*awful*
wonderful   ...*terrible*
leisurely   ...*slowcoach*
glorious   ...*horrible*
up to date   ...*snailpace*
white and shiny...*driving me bonkers*
Stuck behind the man, stuck behind the man
Stuck behind the man with the caravan
That's me   ...*That's him*

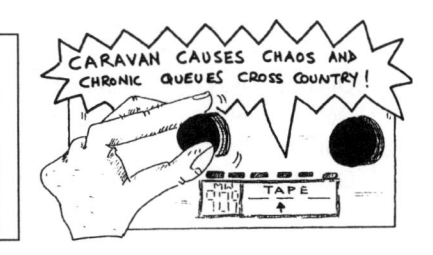

BULLY IN LORRY GET OUT OF MY WAY

Eighteen wheels pounding down the motorway
Eighteen wheels rolling down the road
Eighteen wheels travelling every whichway
Eighteen wheels powering the load

I'm a bully in a lorry and I'm always in a hurry
I'm a bully in a lorry and I never say sorry
I'm a bully in a lorry full of slurry from Bury
I'm a bully in a lorry and I never say sorry

Concrete to Cardiff
Stack of steel to Sunderland
Bags of bricks to Basildon
Rolls of Rags to Rotherham
Out of my way   pedal to the metal
Out of my way   drive drive drive
Out of my way   outside lane
Out of my way   doing 95

Eighteen wheels pounding down the motorway
Eighteen wheels rolling down the road
Eighteen wheels travelling every whichway
Eighteen wheels powering the load

I'm a bully in a lorry and I'm always in a hurry
I'm a bully in a lorry and I never say sorry
I'm a bully in a lorry full of slurry from Bury
I'm a bully in a lorry and I never say sorry

Chicken sheds from Chippenham
Widgets from Warrington
Piles of pipes from Penzance
Tons of tea to Tenby
Out of my way   hammering the tarmac
Out of my way   giving it some gas
Out of my way   thunder down the black track
Out of my way   nobody gets past

I'll wait until you're nearly past
Then move into your lane
I'll make you brake and shake so fast
You won't try it again
I'll flash my lights and sound my horn
Because I own the road
I'm always there in front of you
The long and winding load

Out of my way   pedal to the metal
Out of my way   drive drive drive
Out of my way   outside lane
Out of my way   doing 95
Out of my way   hammering the tarmac
Out of my way   giving it some gas
Out of my way   thunder down the black track
Out of my way   nobody gets past

Eighteen wheels pounding down the motorway
Eighteen wheels rolling down the road
Eighteen wheels travelling every whichway
Eighteen wheels powering the load

I'm a bully in a lorry and I never say sorry
You'd better start to worry cos I'm hotter than a curry
Pounding down the motorway rolling down the road
Travelling every whichway powering the load
Hammering the tarmac giving it some gas
Thunder down the black track nobody gets past
Pedal to the metal drive drive drive
Outside lane 95
GET OUT OF MY WAY

FATHER'S HANDS

Father's hands
large like frying pans
broad as shovel blades
strong as weathered spades.

Father's hands
finger ends ingrained with dirt
permanently stained from work
ignoring pain and scorning hurt.

I once saw him walk boldly up to a swan
that had landed in next door s drive and wouldn't move.
The Police were there because swans are protected species
but didn't do anything but my dad walked up to it,
picked it up and carried it away. No problem.
Those massive wings that can break a man's bones
were held tight, tight by my father's hands
and I was proud of him that day, really proud.

Father's hands
tough as leather on old boots
firmly grasping nettle shoots
pulling thistles by their roots.

Father's hands
gripping like an iron vice
never numb in snow and ice
nails and screws are pulled and prised.

He once found a kestrel with a broken wing
and kept it in the garage until it was better.
He'd feed it by hand with scraps of meat or dead mice
and you could see where its beak and talons
had taken bits of skin from his finger ends.
It never seemed to hurt him at all, he just smiled
as he let it claw and peck.

Father's hands
tossing bales of hay and straw
calloused, hardened, rough and raw
building, planting, painting ... more.

Father's hands
hard when tanning my backside
all we needed they supplied
and still my hands will fit inside
my father's hands
large like frying pans
broad as shovel blades
strong as weathered spades
and still my hands will fit inside
my father's hands.

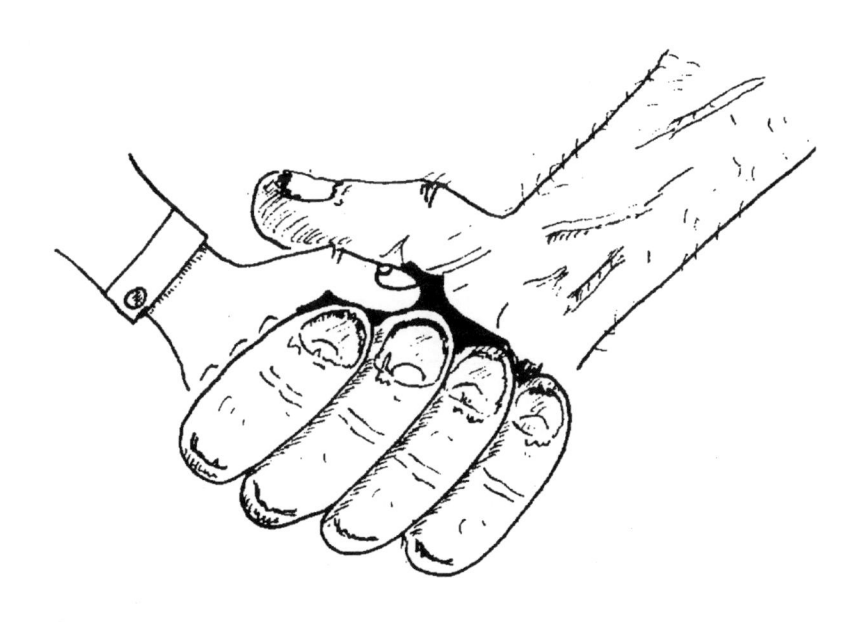

LOSING AT HOME

I never cried when my Grandma died
You see I was away from home at the time
The first time I saw my Grandfather
he was watching World Cup Football on the telly.
He told me that it was a good match and that
the goalie had made some fantastic saves
although we were still one nil down.
But somewhere behind his eyes
a light had dimmed
and on the other side of his glasses
I could see teardrops forming
and as they fell down his face
they weren't because
his team had lost
but because he had lost
his team.

You see, to my Grandfather
my Grandmother was his best team
in the world.
Ever.

WINTER MORNING: WINTER NIGHT

This morning I walked to school
through the dark
it was so cold my shadow shivered
under the street lamps.

My feet cracked the ice
that glittered as hard as the frosted stars
stuck on the sky's blue back.

Cars crept by like giant cats
their bright eyes shining.

Tonight I walked over the snow
the moon's cool searchlight
splashed its glow over the garden.

Picking out details of rooftops and hedges
as clearly and sharply
as a summer stillness just after dawn.

Cars on the street roared like lions
bounding over the wet tarmac.

WITH HER TROLLEY AND HER BROLLY AND HER PLASTIC BAGS

Every week come rain or shine Granny goes into town
With her trolley and her brolly and her plastic bags
No-ones safe around
Crash! Bang! Wallop! Ouch!
Crash! Bang! Wallop! Ouch!

Mothers, fathers, children, pets, all of them walk faster
With her trolley and her brolly and her plastic bags
Granny's a disaster
Crash! Bang! Wallop! Ouch!
Crash! Bang! Wallop! Ouch!

She moans about the prices to every shopping stranger
With her trolley and her brolly and her plastic bags
Everyone's in danger
Crash! Bang! Wallop! Ouch!
Crash! Bang! Wallop! Ouch!

Half a dozen apples
She puts them in one bag   ...ONE
Two loaves of bread
She puts them in one bag   ...TWO
A pair of knee length bloomers
She puts them in one bag   ...THREE
Glue for her false teeth
She puts them in one bag   ...FOUR
A bungee jumping outfit
She puts them in one bag   ...FIVE
A Luton town away kit
She puts them in one bag   ...SIX
Bazooka and tank
She puts them in one bag   ...SEVEN

Shopping bags like boxing gloves with tins and frozen chops
With her trolley and her brolly and her plastic bags
Like Rambo at the shops
Crash! Bang! Wallop! Ouch!
Crash! Bang! Wallop! Ouch!

"When I was young" she says
"Things were different then"
With her trolley and her brolly and her plastic bags
She knocked down sixteen men
Crash! Bang! Wallop! Ouch!
Crash! Bang! Wallop! Ouch!

So watch out for my Granny on your shopping spree
With her trolley and her brolly and her plastic bags
She'd win world war three
Crash! Bang! Wallop! Ouch!
Crash! Bang! Wallop! Ouch!
Crash! Bang! Wallop! Ouch!
Crash! Bang! Wallop! .... **Ouch!**

SHIRLEY AND CHARLOTTE THE SHELL SUIT SISTERS

Shirley and Charlotte the shell suit sisters
Swish swish swisherty swish
Swishing shell suits shiny and silver
Swish swish swisherty swish
Shirley's shell suit's short and shabby
Swish swish swisherty swish
Charlotte's shell suit shines and shimmers
Swish swish swisherty swish

Printed pink and purple patterns
Red and wrinkled zip up tops
Black and blue baggy bottoms
Dazzling white new Reeboks

See them glint and see them glimmer
Sparkling in the Summer sun
If you're fat or if you're thinner
One size fits everyone!

Shirley and Charlotte the shell suit sisters
Swish etc. etc.

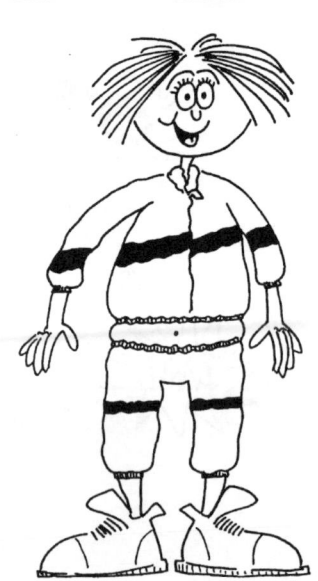

Zips that dangle zips that jangle
Kilometres of elastic
Round your wrists and round your ankles
Pulling so tight that it's drastic

So restricting and constricting
Hands and ankles blue and green
Faces turning red and purple
Which is shell suit which is skin?

Shirley and Charlotte the shell suit sisters
Swish etc. etc.

Do the shell suit shimmy with Shirley and Charlotte
Shiver and shake side to side
Do the shell suit shimmy with Shirley and Charlotte
Shiver and shake slip and slide

Shirley and Charlotte the shell suit sisters
Swish etc. etc.

FA RULES OK

Life isn't easy in our house
My dad's a referee
He's always right, never wrong
And he knows all the rules

Every day he comes home
Shiny black shirt
Shiny black shorts
Shiny red face
Shiny silver whistle

He races around the house
Checking the nets on the curtains
The height of the crossbars over the doors

He doesn't like it
When the budgie talks back to him
He gets mad when the dog
Dribbles down his leg
And he booked the cat for spitting

If we don't wash our hands before tea
That's it - a warning
Leaving our greens - yellow card
Giving them to the dog - red card

Being sent off in your own house
Is no fun
It's a long lonely walk upstairs
For that early bath
Early bed, no telly
And no extra time

Yes, life isn't easy in our house
Dad's always right
And he knows all the rules

GIVING THEIR GOALIE BACKACHE

It's brilliant, ace and great
Wednesday evening I can't wait
Hit the field with the ball
I can hear them shout and call
On the touchline, drive me crazy
My class yelling "Come on Tracy!
Come on girl
Make it flick, swerve and curl
Make it dip, make it shimmer
The other day you scored the winner
The week before you made them sick
Sticking in your hat trick
So don't you hesitate
This week we want eight"

We haven't been like other teams
Broken hearts and broken dreams
Losing games and leagues and cups
Seasons full of downs not ups
But then I got the knack
The feel, the bug, the bite,
My teacher moved me to attack
And now we're dynamite

It's brilliant, great and ace
You should see their goalie's face
I knocked it in, hit the net
The other team were so upset
When they arrived the silly crowd
Had looked at me and laughed out loud
Because I was a girl
But I can make it spin and whirl
Use both feet, use my head
Leave their centre-back for dead
Drive it through so we score
And all the time the crowd shout MORE
I did not hesitate
That match we got eight

THE INVENTOR'S HOUSE

Professor McFizzer's a very strange fellow
Bright purple smoke and brilliant yellow
Flashes of light jump, gurgle and pour
Out of his windows and under his door.

When he's inventing the whole street shakes
Feels like we're having a dozen earthquakes
He thumps and he hammers clatters and yells
Causing explosions and very bad smells.

He invented a tent that doesn't need poles
A new fishing-net that doesn't need holes
He invented a pencil that never once broke
And see-through false teeth just for a joke.

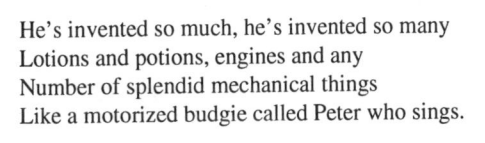

He's invented so much, he's invented so many
Lotions and potions, engines and any
Number of splendid mechanical things
Like a motorized budgie called Peter who sings.

Last night a large rocket whooshed through the sky
He was there at the wheel learning to fly
He's as mad as a March hare out for adventure
Professor McFizzer our famous inventor.

This can be fun for audience participation. The section in italics "Two parts jam..." etc can be taught and repeated in each verse by the group
For the chorus divide the group in half. One half can be the pigs and make an Oink! while the others can be the muck and make a Slurp!

HAPPY AS A PIG IN MUCK

I once knew a man as sad as can be
stung on the bum by a bumble bee.
He had to stand for a week or two
couldn't sit down on the loo.
He wrote away for a miracle cure
and four days later through his door
there came a list and letter
saying "Do this and get better".
He followed the instructions
creating this concoction.
A most exotic potion
A strange and weird lotion ...
It was two parts jam, one part cream,
beans, greens, tangerines,
all stirred up with a great big stick
and twice a day spread on thick
He spread it on, rubbed it in
and could not believe his luck.
The potion worked, the pain had gone
and now he's happy as a pig in muck

Happy as a pig ***Oink! Slurp!***
Happy as a pig ***Oink! Slurp!***
Happy as a pig ***Oink! Slurp!***
Happy as a pig in muck

The man knew a boy, name of Lee
who hadn't smiled since he was three.
A face as long as an ironing board
he never ventured out of doors.
Sat in a chair dawn till dusk
a glassy stare collecting dust.
A terminally awful frown
like a banana upside down.
The man said "I know what to do,
it worked for me and will for you".

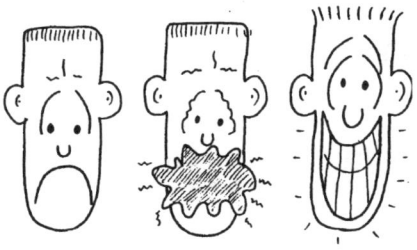

A most exotic potion
A strange and weird lotion ...
It was two parts jam, one part cream,
beans, greens, tangerines,
all stirred up with a great big stick
and twice a day spread on thick
He spread it on, rubbed it in
and could not believe his luck.
The frown had gone, he smiled again
and now he's happy as a pig in muck

Happy as a pig *Oink! Slurp! ... etc*

Happy as a pig *Oink! Slurp! ... etc*

So if you're feeling very ill, remember this will make you well
Follow this discovery to aid your own recovery
A most exotic potion, a strange and weird lotion
It was two parts jam, one part cream, beans, greens, tangerines,
all stirred up with a great big stick and twice a day spread on thick
So spread it on, rub it in and you will not believe your luck
The potion works and you will be - as happy as a pig in muck

Happy as a pig *Oink! Slurp! ... etc.*

FROM PONTEFRACT TO DONCASTER

When I lived in Pontefract it was a shift system.
It was the only way to get anyone to live there.
I was on the 1984 to 1989 shift
working in a school by day
and in the liquorice fields at night.

It wasn't soft Southern liquorice
It was rough tough Northern stuff,
a root crop made of wood.
Hard work and if you weren't careful
you'd get splinters in your fingernails.
There was an industrial injury peculiar to Pontefract:
Lickrishbum.
What happened was that over the time the splinters
passed through your body and years later a lump
the exact size and shape of half a pound of liquorice allsorts
would appear on your left bum.
Old lads would hobble around Pontefract
unable to sit down for weeks
until the condition passed,
especially if it was a double pounder
- one on each cheek,
or even worse that with the red and blue spots on.

I didn't mind my shift in Pontefract that much
but they're mean with their cakes
In Eccles and Dundee you get a good cake.
In Chorley and Battenburg you get a splendid cake.
The ones that come from Pontefract are small, hard
and stink of liquorice.
And that's just the people.

After that I moved to Doncaster.
I like living in exciting places as you can tell.
I start at the Butterscotch Mines tomorrow.
You can tell which ones they are ...
they're still open.

DO YOU KNOW ARNIE'S NEW FILM WHERE GALLONS OF TOXIC WASTE AND RADIO ACTIVE CHEMICALS SPILL ONTO AN ALLOTMENT AFFECTING ALL THE CREATURES IN THE SOIL SO THAT THEY MUTATE INTO GIANT BLOODSUCKING MONSTERS?
HMM... NO WHICH ONE'S THAT?
WORMINATOR!

WORMINATOR

TRAINSPOTTER

125
Trainspotter trainspotter trainspotter train train   X2

He's got the anorak, he's got the duffle bag
The big note book and pocket full of pens
Fountain pens and cartridge pens
And all those flipping biros
Yes all those flipping biros

Cos Derek's ready Derek's ready Derek's ready Derek's ready
For the red light orange light green light GO!

Whoosh! Missed it.

Trainspotter trainspotter trainspotter train train   X2

He's got the sandwiches, he's got the thermos flask
Family pack of crisps and a pocket full of sweets
Chocolate bars and Yorkie bars
And all those flipping Penguins
Yes all those flipping Penguins

Cos Derek's ready Derek's ready Derek's ready Derek's ready
For the red light orange light green light GO!

Whoosh! Missed it.

Have another go have another go
Get a closer look get a closer look
At the red light orange light green light GO!

Caught it right in the back right in the back
Right in the back of the anorak
So now they're spotting Derek
So now they're spotting Derek

Trainspotter trainspotter trainspotter train train   X2
They've got the anorak that's in Crewe
The sandwiches they're in Wick
The big note book that's loose-leaf
Covers all the regions covers all the regions
Mind you so does Derek
Mind you so does Derek

With his red light orange light green light GO!

Trainspotter trainspotter trainspotter train train   X2
NEEOWN

THE MAN WITH FOUR CHINS

He's the man (Huh!)
The man with four chins
Watch them wobble like washing in the wind
He's the man (huh!)
The man with four chins
Flapping folding flesh and skin
Watch them wobble - 1 2 3 4!
Watch them wobble - 1 2 3 4!
Watch them wobble - 1 2 3 4!
The man with 1 2 3 4 chins!

Like a sweater with a polo neck
ten times a normal size
or inner tubes inflating
from four tractor tyres
Who's that man with a head like a bubble?
He's the man whose double chin's a double!

Look at that! Well flippin' eck!
There goes a bloke who's got no neck!
You can't tell where his body stops and where his head begins!
You can't tell where his body stops and where his head begins!

He's the man etc.

Facial hills and valleys
he's the only man that I know
who has to shave three times a day
with a strimmer and a flymo
You can bet your bottom dollar
it's the man whose chins cover his collar

Look at that! Well flippin' eck!
There goes a bloke who's got no neck!
You can't tell where his body stops and where his head begins!
You can't tell where his body stops and where his head begins!

He's the man etc.

Who needs an Ordnance Survey Map just to find his lips?
Whose jowls make you howl and hang down to his hips?
Who could never put the shot because of all the chins he's got?
Who'll never play the violin because it won't fit under his chin?
Who's the man whose face expands and wobbles when he grins?
Who's the man with the vast expanse of glands around his chins?

Look at that! Well flippin' eck!
There goes a bloke who's got no neck!
You can't tell where his body stops and where his head begins!
You can't tell where his body stops and where his head begins!

He's the man etc.

THE AMAZING CAPTAIN CONCORDE

IS IT A BIRD?
IS IT A PLANE?
LOOK AT THE SIZE OF THE NOSE ON HIS FACE!
IS IT A BIRD?
IS IT A PLANE?
CAPTAIN CONCORDE IS HIS NAME!
CAPTAIN CONCORDE NEEEEOOWN!
CAPTAIN CONCORDE NEEEEOOWN!

A man with a mission
Radar vision
A nose that's supersonic
Faster than the speed of sound
His Y fronts are bionic
Big and baggy
Red and saggy
Streamlined underpants
Always ready
Hi tech sheddies
Crooks don't stand a chance

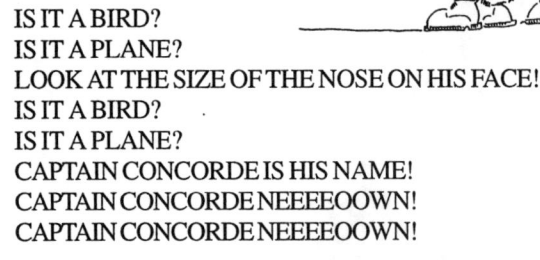

IS IT A BIRD?
IS IT A PLANE?
LOOK AT THE SIZE OF THE NOSE ON HIS FACE!
IS IT A BIRD?
IS IT A PLANE?
CAPTAIN CONCORDE IS HIS NAME!
CAPTAIN CONCORDE NEEEEOOWN!
CAPTAIN CONCORDE NEEEEOOWN!

Anytime anyplace anywhere
But never ever Mondays
Coz that's the day the Captain's mum
Washes his red undies

Anytime anyplace anywhere
His power is fantastic
Everthing's under control
With super strength elastic

Anytime anyplace anywhere
But bathrooms are a no no
Coz the toilet seat has teeth OW!
And then it's time to go so ...

IS IT A BIRD?
IS IT A PLANE?
LOOK AT THE SIZE OF THE NOSE ON HIS FACE!
IS IT A BIRD?
IS IT A PLANE?
CAPTAIN CONCORDE IS HIS NAME!
CAPTAIN CONCORDE NEEEEOOWN!
CAPTAIN CONCORDE NEEEEOOWN!

The Amazing Captain Concorde ... he's a superman.
The Amazing Captain Concorde ... super underpants
The Amazing Captain Concorde ... nobody can trick him
The Amazing Captain Concorde ... with a nose like that you'd pick him.

Who's the man with the supersonic nose?................... Captain Concorde!
Who's the man with horrible taste in clothes?..............Captain Concorde!
Who's the man who's always your best friend? ....Captain Concorde!
Who's the man who's always set the trend? .... Captain Concorde!
Who's the man who's so aerodynamic? ....Captain Concorde!
Who's the man who makes the villains panic? .... Captain Concorde!
Who's the man who always helps his mum? ....Captain Concorde!
Who's the man you'd all like to become? ....Captain Concorde!
Who? Captain Concorde!
Who? Captain Concorde!
So ...

IS IT A BIRD?
IS IT A PLANE?
LOOK AT THE SIZE OF THE NOSE ON HIS FACE!
IS IT A BIRD?
IS IT A PLANE?
CAPTAIN CONCORDE IS HIS NAME!
CAPTAIN CONCORDE NEEEEOOWN!
CAPTAIN CONCORDE NEEEEOOWN!

WHAT ON EARTH HAPPENED TO MY LITTLE SISTER HAYLEY ANN?

I'm very worried about my little sister Hayley Ann.
The strangest things have started happening.

She's only seven years old
but already she's grown a bright blue beard.
Weird!

Her ears are now pointed
and glow red, amber and green like traffic lights.
What a sight!

She doesn't have a nose,
it's more like a trunk or a vacuum cleaner
and she just goes round sucking up anything and everything
from dust and hairs and jellies, spiders webs,
dad's slippers and the dog's food with a squelchy slurp.
Then she burps!

Her eyes are as big as golf balls
and stuck on stalks all round her head.
She has seven of them so she can see through the week
Freaky!

She teleports from room to room
leaving little showers of rainbow sparks behind her
that fade away and simply disappear.
We don't see her!

Her mouth is now a computer screen
flashing bright green messages.
She has a joystick on her chin
and a keyboard on her shoulder.
We have to decode her!

Yes I'm very worried about my little sister.
I mean she's even started spelling her name differently.
It's now A - L - and I - E - N.
I think my little sister Hayley Ann is really an ...
ALIEN!!

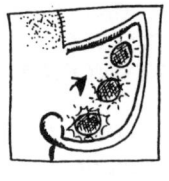

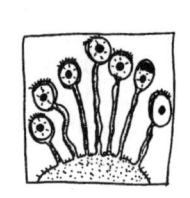

RIBOFLAVIN

SNAP CRACKLE POP POP POP
SNAP CRACKLE POP POP POP

Every morning in your bowl
A flake of sunshine to fill your soul
Every chunk you have to chew
Looks and tastes like used up glue
Clogging the insides of you
With red and green revolting goo
I don't want to get polemical
But all of it is one big chemical

THIAMIN NIACIN VITAMIN VYTAMIN
THIAMIN NIACIN VITAMIN VYTAMIN
HAVE A BRAIN LIGHT AGAIN
HAVE AN EYE BRIGHT AGAIN
GRAB ANOTHER BITE OF
RIBOFLAVIN ... LOTSA GOLDEN CORN
RIBOFLAVIN ... LOTSA GOLDEN CORN
RIBOFLAVIN ... LOTSA GOLDEN CORN

SNAP CRACKLE POP POP POP
SNAP CRACKLE POP POP POP

They do such things with corn
A flipping great cockerel on your lawn
A whole gang of kids you've never seen
All by appointment to the Queen
Bet she keeps her inside clean
With all that iron and protein
Watching companies getting wealthier
When eating the cardboard would be healthier

THIAMIN NIACIN VITAMIN VYTAMIN ETC.

TO THE PORK PIE

Oh pork pie, oh pie of pork
Let there be no mean mouthed talk
About fat content, gristle, grease
The dangers of turning obese
Your pastry gleams, your jelly quivers
My saliva flows in rivers.
I love your shining, lardy case
You're ace.

Oh pie of pork, oh pork pie
I don't deceive, lie or deny
When I declare my love, my passion
Is for more than my fair ration
Of your succulence and splendour
Your crunchy crust and meat so tender
I see you waiting on my plate
You're great.

I'm the fall guy for my pork pie
A pasty patsy who will try
On the sly stalking by
To spot and spy that special pie
In motorway shop or supermarket
That satisfying pie's my target
Snatch it down from the cold shelf
Consume its glories all by myself
Savour every crumb and swallow
Hope to eat three more tomorrow

Oh pork pie, oh pork pie
I tell you friend my fork is nigh
I feel you glide though my strong jaws
Your plump girth, your rolling contours
Piquant taste and chewy texture
Fills my mouth up with an extra
Tasty gormandising thrill
You're brill.

WHAT CLASS 4 FEAR THE MOST

We wish our teacher
Would not push
His pencil in his ear.

Not the sharp bit
But the blunt bit
It's the moment we all fear.

He wiggles it
He jiggles it
Turns it round and round.

Then pulls it out
With a squidgy slurp
Looks at what he's found.

Sometimes it's runny
Like golden honey
Dripping on his tie.

Or brown as coffee
Like sticky toffee
Crusty as a pie.

First he sniffs it
Then he licks it
Wipes it on his sleeve.

Then uses it
To mark our sums
Makes our stomach heave.

More Dinosaurs That Time Forgot

The beach loving dinosaur .... the Sandyshorus

The uncertain dinosaur .... the NowI'mnotsosurus

The high rise dinosaur .... the Multistorysaurus

The home help dinosaur .... the Householdchorasurus

The short-sighted dinosaur .... the Tyrannosaurus Specs

The hooligan dinosaur .... the Tyrannosaurus Wrecks

The weightlifting dinosaur .... the Tyrannosaurus Pecks

The dinosaurs who loves Chinese food .... the Friedriceratops and Sweetandsourporkasaurus

The law enforcing dinosaur .... the Triceracops

The magical dinosaur .... the Diplohocuspokus

The blurred dinosaur .... the Diplo-outoffocus

The dinosaur that likes bonfires .... Diplochokasmokus

The flying dinosaur that's always late .... the Terrywon'tbebacktill

The drunken flying dinosaur .... the Verymerrydactyl

The farming dinosaur .... the Velocitractor

The dinosaur that's pulled a muscle .... the Velocirupture

PERCY IS A PUNK

1 2 3 4 Daggadaggadaggadagga! (X4)

Percy is a punk OY! (X4)

1 2 3 4 Daggadaggadaggadagga! (X4)

Percy is a punk OY! (X4)

Give us a   P!....P!
Give us an   E!....E!
Give us an   R!....R!
Give us a   C!....C!
Give us a   Y!....Y!

What does that spell?   Percy!

1 2 3 4 Daggadaggadaggadagga! (X4)

Percy is a punk OY! (X4)

Percy is a
Percy is a
Percy is a .... PUNK! OY!

ROCKER ON A PUSHBIKE

Rocker on a push bike Roller with a pedal
The frame on his bike is very heavy metal
No bell on his handlebar
Instead he's got an electric guitar
Bambambaa Bambambabaa Bambambaa Bambaa !

Has no bike clips on his legs, wears them on his ears instead.
Tyres painted black and white, psychedelic flashing lights.
Bike chain makes a racket on the back of his leather jacket.
Gears dry up and need repair, rubs them down with greasy hair.

Rocker on a push bike ... etc.

Cool cat leaders of the pack, everyone knows when the boys are back
Justin, Jeremy, Robin, Michael, these are the boys born to cycle.
Speed kings live for thrills except when they go up the hills.
Feel the speed, see the power, nearly at one mile an hour.

Rocker on a push bike ... etc.

Rockers rollers heavy sweaty wrecks
Knock kneed bozos on a B.M.X.
Pedal pedal heavy metal pedal
Heavy metal pedal on a B.M.X.
Pedal pedal heavy metal pedal
Knock kneed heavy sweaty wrecks
Pedal pedal heavy metal pedal
Too much beer and cigarettes
Pedal pedal heavy metal pedal
Pointy boots and leather kecks
Pedal pedal heavy metal pedal
Heavy metal pedal on a B.M.X.
Heavy metal pedal on a B.M.X.

Rocker on a push bike .. etc.

SPILL THE BEANS

Paul Cookson and David Harmer

*"In their unique performance
Spill The Beans bring out the child in
every adult and the adult in every child."*
Nick Toczek, Bradford Festival

David Harmer and Paul Cookson also work together as Spill The Beans - a performance poetry act for all the family.

A lively entertaining show can be guaranteed with laughs, high speed performance poetry and plenty of audience participation.
Together they have performed thousands of shows at thousands of venues.

As experienced teachers they have also organised hundreds of work shops for all ages as well as numerous In Service Courses and training for teachers, librarians and others.

For further information and bookings write (with S.A.E.) to:

Spill The Beans
P.O. Box 25
Retford
Notts DN22 7ER

BOOKS AVAILABLE FROM "A TWIST IN THE TALE"

The Toilet Seat Has Teeth	Illustrated poems by Paul Cookson £3.95 (incl. p&p)
Over 21 And Still Into Noddy	Selected poems 1979 - 91 by Paul Cookson Intro by Noddy Holder £5.35 (incl. p&p)
Spill The Beans	Illustrated poems by Paul Cookson & David Harmer £3.95 (incl. p&p)
Rhyming Rhythms For Twisted Tongues	Illustrated poems by Paul Cookson £3.95 (incl. p&p)
Creaking Down The Corridor	Poems by David Harmer Illustrated by Paul Cookson £3.95 (incl. p&p)
Secret Staffrooms And Crazy Classrooms	The Spill The Beans Guide to Schools by Paul Cookson and David Harmer £3.95 (incl. p&p)
Spill The Beans Badges	50p each (incl. p&p)
Captain Concorde Badges	50p each (incl. p&p)

Available from:
A TWIST IN THE TALE, P.O. BOX 25, RETFORD, NOTTS, DN22 7ER

Please make all cheques and postal orders payable to "A TWIST IN THE TALE"
Allow 28 days for delivery